C000001875

After Effects

poems by

Judith Janoo

Finishing Line Press
Georgetown, Kentucky

After Effects

For Louise Rader

ACKNOWLEDGMENTS

I wish to thank the following where poems were originally published or recognized:

"Beaches of Normandy," *Evening Street Review*, finalist for Dana Award
"The Hay Barn," *Evening Street Review*
"Struck," first appeared in *The Main Street Rag*
"Buddleia," won the Soul Making Keats Award, finalist for the Dana
    Award, first appeared in *The Main Street Rag*
"Nets," *Deadly Writers Patrol*, Reader's Choice Poetry Society of VT
"Regret," first appeared in *The Main Street Rag*
"What You Passed On," *Deadly Writers Patrol*
"Song," first appeared in *The Main Street Rag*, finalist for Dana Award
"Independence Day," first appeared in *The Main Street Rag*
"The Edge of the Gorge," published in *Pedestal Magazine*, won the Goldstein
    Memorial Award
"Mike," won the Laura J. Spooner Memorial Award, published in *The
    Mountain Troubadour*
"Shoreline," appeared at "Poem City"
"Salmo, GMO," won the Chris White Memorial Award, published in *The
    Mountain Troubadour*
"Snow Travels," *The Mountain Troubadour*
"Moonslide," *Euphony Journal*
"Stacking Wood," *Vermont Magazine*, finalist for Ralph Nading Hill Award
"Take To The Streets, Feb. 15, 2003" *Evening Street Review*, won the Anita
    McAndrews Award for human rights poetry
"We Wanted Color Not to Matter," *The Mountain Troubadour*
"Chaing Mai, City of Temples," *PoemCity*
"The Owl's Gaze," *Poem Town*

Publisher: Leah Maines
Editor: Christen Kincaid
Cover Art: Rosalie Vear
Author Photo: SJ Cahill
Cover Design: Leah Huete

Printed in the USA on acid-free paper.
Order online: www.finishinglinepress.com
        also available on amazon.com

Author inquiries and mail orders:
Finishing Line Press
P. O. Box 1626
Georgetown, Kentucky 40324
U. S. A.

Table of Contents

The Department of War

The Ministry of Peace

In 1793 Benjamin Rush, a U.S. founding father and signer of the Declaration of Independence proposed the plan of a Peace-Office of the United States. In 1935 Senator Matthew M. Neely introduced the first bill calling for the creation of a United States Department of Peace. Similar bills have been introduced into the legislature—the latest: The Department of Peace Act of 2011, reintroduced in 2013.

The Department of War

What You Passed On

Reading yourself to sleep,
early morning on the water
hauling mackerel from a dory,
        midday

felling birches, firs, leaving
the red oak arching
over the cove.
        You left us:

your bronze medal,
an American flag,
German lugers,
        your army green cap.

On the shelf you left:
ocean manuals to show us
fish have no lids—their eyes
        always open,

forestry books, how to graft
fruit trees, transplant a cedar,
save a deciduous tree
        struck by lightning.

Between *Poems of Wilfred Owen*
and *All The King's Men*
you left a signed copy
        of *Mein Kampf*

you must have had
reason to keep
like the memory
      you didn't know

what to do with
once you brought
      it home.

Nets

A southwest wind
brings mackerel
into the cove, dawn
opening rose-gold
over a seiner's net,
under scree of gulls,
under cormorant shadows
landing on dories.
Mackerel smell
thick as engine oil.
Whoosh of net as he pulls
arms-lengths, drops
silver heads, tails,
metallic blue-green backs
curled as hooks
fighting entrapment,
the man-made tide
washing them
from their pocket
of ocean.

***

Gentle boy in army fatigues
enters the English Channel,
in combat boots
descends rope net, crosses
Omaha Beach. No southwest wind
to guide him past dragon's teeth,
up the looming bluff,
his back silver with sweat
from tainted yellow-fever
vaccine. He makes it beyond fire, blast
beyond the past that drafted him
into this war,

sees in the darkness
the noiseless pulse of mackerel,
phosphorescent schools
swimming inshore.

**

The cove, red-orange,
teeming with fish,
he reaches for the net
as from a rooftop,
as from blindness of night,
from a cliff, draws the net
over the gunnel of his dory.
Mackerel slip down
into the hull with
what's left of him,
the worst that he knows,
vows never to repeat.
He oils his hands with scales,
V-shaped tails as glazed,
lidless eyes
stare up at him.

Beaches of Normandy

Crossing coves, clasping rope
hand-over-hand, crossing beaches
of gunfire; fishermen, farmers,
teachers turned soldiers,

turned onto beaches of gunfire,
gentle men, enlisted men, the drafted,
their landing craft wind-shifted,
water-mined in iron pieces off beaches

of gunfire; foot soldiers fog-blinded,
facing beaches land-mined, staked,
barb-wired; foot soldiers facing aerial fire,
the enemy's and their own, clearing

beaches for amphibious landings. Souls
crying for leaders lost to sea, seeing ahead
only bodies, embankment, beaches of
gunfire with no choice but to advance.

And the man I knew who made it
up the bluff of Omaha Beach,
never really cleared the beaches
of gunfire. Nights, his bottle

half empty, he aired
the start of it and I'd listen,
then hear him pace the hall
outside my room,

sweating out the dead he failed
to save, crossed to mount
the looming bluff, a shooting
duck out of water without a chance

in hell of making it, varsity runner
not wounding even a deer
until on the beaches of gunfire
he outran the worst of it

and kept running.

The Owl's Gaze

We cleared the dining room table;
stacks of news, German ivy cuttings
rooted in peat and vermiculite
beneath the dusty, snowy owl

perched on the china cabinet,
above heirlooms of blue
willowware, chipped, crazed,
passed down and saved.

This room was our path to the yard
rimmed with honeysuckle berries
waxwings dropped like cherry Jell-O
against the window to Dad

fumbling open his buffet drawer
of seized Lugers, kept private
except to show chosen visitors
in this room where we knew not

to linger, save occasions when
we'd arrange the cherished
dishes, nervous they'd fracture
under the shadow of the hooked

beak, the imprint of wings
in cranberry sauce, on buffet
drawer, the narrow eyes
of the hunter, defender

fixed beyond us,
beyond the owlets
sent out to open wings
to the darkness,

not to feast as the raven,
but to *gahw*
and swallow whole

and to later
digest the pieces.

Struck

Hope is the thing with feathers
—Emily Dickinson

If you see him seated
beneath the ash tree he
saved, painted boat gray

after lightning struck, split,
taking half the high branches
leaving one side shade,

you'll see the warbler,
her nest invaded
with cowbird eggs

she must bury, and her
own, weave a new tier
of deer hair and feathers

that spill hope on the soldier,
fused to the ash umbrella,
to lasting combat

and might understand
what it takes for him
to look at you,

the glare too much
for his severed side
you've tried to keep

from falling.

The Dowser

I watch my father
hold the apple branch
against Earth's draw,

his muscled hands
and wrists resist
the splayed limb's thirst,

trembling with the soldier
who in the noise and fog
shouted where to run

before taken down.
But spared, my father
now taps the deep well,

his scarred wood scouting
a drilling spot for neighbors
whose well has gone dry.

Slender rod parched,
wrenches his shoulders,
until spent, convinced,

he releases the bough.
And hands it to me.
Can you feel it?

My palms strained,
quivering, I brace against
the connection to the vein,

to my father
or some part of him.

Tracks

Let a slight snow come...show how little the woods and fields are frequented.
—Thoreau

The air wrings itself out
    snow-sharp cold
over fissured fields.

I follow first signs of a canine
    meandering toward pines.
Further into spruce,

an owl has touched down
    on powder, swooped
across the surface like a rake.

Deer hooves trace straight
    along their corridor.
First human in the storm,

sound only of snow
    filling rabbit prints,
loading branches that let go

snowblinks of father's tracks
    across France to Sudetenland,
great rooms I never filled,

moonless caves
    draped with arms carved
into deep-weighted

hollows
    I sink into until
the impression

vanishes.

Tinsel

First the string of lights,
each balsam limb given

a crimson, blue-green hue.
The handmade ornaments:

chestnuts painted with Santa faces,
felt bells, crocheted snow flakes

neatly placed, and finally
the star; cardboard, foiled,

set at needled apex to reflect
the luster she plugged in,

signaling us to hang the tinsel,
one silver strand at a time,

while she tended the gingerbread,
plumping in the oven, molasses wafting

from the kitchen until he came in.
The door's leather-strung bells

rang as he reached for my tinsel tray.
Regiment unbearable, he flung

a silver fistful that landed
on one branch. I convinced myself

he meant to add festivity.

Second Cutting

The sun unpacks its glare
on the field's timothy
yellowing into brown

toasting new-baled hay
tawny as the briar root pipe
clamped between his teeth

his army cap faded tan
long after his landing
on Normandy

believing there was no
making it
but making it

making me believe
unceasing vigilance
will lift pipe smoke

beyond bobolink's nest
in the uncut grass
at tractor's edge

lift it beyond
the clover beyond
me barefoot

bending over
to save
one

four-leafed green

The Sparrow and the Lily

I learned fear
stamped cold

as winter glass,
velocity my shield.

I dissolved
in the face of it,

faced up to it, and
left myself behind

to face it later.
Dreams of triumph

silenced in a soldier's
anguish. Fear

swallowed my worth,
locked it inside

burning like fresh ash,
smell of old salami,

boneless marrow
squalling for solace,

distant stillness
mirrored in shards,

gathered by
the sparrow

and the lily feeding
from the field.

Song

Apple blossoms falling
into bowls of verses
our parents learned
in the Depression,
carried with them
through Iwo Jima
and Normandy when
hearing was believing.

But we traded our radios
for TV trays, watched Tet
Offensive, Baghdad, flashes
of shadowed truths, our ears
no longer mirrors,

we longed for still waters,
imagined heroes,
green pastures to rest in.
Yeah though I walk
through the valley
of my father's shadow
a song forms itself
to the bowl I stroke
round and round its rim,
wanting to be filled
still waiting to be filled.

Regret

after dusk, after cool wounded
traces of gray take shape
and reshape the sky above us,

unnoticed in their effortless changings,
dreams we dreamed when we were young,
full of rose and chaste tones, wanting it all

good, world-bettering. We questioned Eve
getting Adam into it, if she was warned
of the voice of harm, she with faith,

the one blamed, first to bite, to probe
the unknown, the faceless as we did
driving west, rebuilt engines taking us

far from the cause of Vietnam, far
from cries of the returned, the injured,
the windless voices against senselessness

we saw needed reshaping, meeting a world
we once ignored, that needed piecing,
as we needed a country to believe in,

to feel safe in. No one warned
of the horrors, no one said
there are those who mean to kill.

Regret—the silence, the smoke
rising from chimneys, homes
with closed doors, chill air

we shake off when we're tired
enough to forget our dream,
forget the shape, the fire inside it.

Surrender

His hospital room white as his thin cotton cover,
the VA nurse pours solution from a blue gallon jug.

Tastes like gun metal, my father says. *How much more*
Roto-Rooter do I have to drink before they cut?

Other infantrymen murmur in clouded rooms
while outside his window water lilies float

on the moon-blue surface of the pond. Petals like swans
misting fresh cream from Monet's water garden in Giverny,

where he rendered degrees of light, until his vision veiled
the soft blues, like the jug my father finishes despite his resolve

to take not a single military handout, be any part of remembering.
This day, the most time we'd ever spent or spoken, I watch

his frozen will dissolve into the water lily white of the nurse's
uniform,
her soft shoes, the outline of her kind blue eyes, onto the stretcher

I walk beside down the long white hall. Smell of Betadine
boring into the darkness like our roots.

My teeth are in the cup by the hospital sink,
he says. *Will you be there when I come out?*

Buddleia

Spring, your Buddleia bush
again strobes pink and white—
a butterfly magnet,

countless pearl crescents, cloudys,
elfins, delicate flapping wings
keeping them aloft.

You thought you'd miss this crop
after the hospice doctor said
six months,

but it's been twenty-four,
longer than you fought
across Europe,

not counting the sixty years
after, war waging still
inside you.

Now you sit on the porch swing,
and I beside you, sometimes
for hours,

no longer do you jump up and leave
when I walk into the room,
and I, no longer

the child who thought
it was my fault your
restlessness.

The Hay Barn

had a loft, a swallow perch, and if we rushed
in, the birds whipped past us, wings parting us,

parting the peace we came for. The old barn
no longer housing lambs or calves. No hay even.

I'd look up after the birds dispersed and see
the Sistine Chapel in the high beams,

thick oak shoulders etched in red as if the builder
lay on his back sealing them in place

to reveal their exact purpose—keeping sheep,
seaming the roof's slant where raindrops crawled

down, dampening the images that grew as I sat
back on my elbows with you, brother,

younger, stronger, more tender inside.
You, the hand-hewn beams of the barn,

the oaks that had grown as arching towers
along the shore, that gave us shelter when the anger,

distanced in the hay-dry space we lay in,
blew over us, over the lingering scent

of pine shavings, faint milkweed
and caraway. This was our escape.

Broad and strong, the solid one
who stayed in place, would not give way

when all you had was taken. I saw
in you etchings of angelic figures,

their raiment wearing away
your exhaust

until your rafters opened.

Mike

The ice cracked and echoed
when we were
young and skating on our father's pond,
as usual,
scratching eights, long into dark.
You heard
the crash as a patch under me gave way.
Quick-thinking
you spied a birch pole. "Hold on," you said,
pulling me to safety,
shattering the frozen surface between us.

***

A fog hangs over the pond, my first time
back since
your heart stopped, chamber by chamber,
while I begged
for transplant or stainless steel.
Faithful brother,
The same pair of Canada geese
you saved
from the weasel watch over
their nest
in the cattails and reeds.

Independence Day

Peonie's bursting sphere,
Horsetail's fire sparks,
fizzles, Rings within Rings,
Chrysanthemums in night sky,
Fountains, Roman Candles
like hot air balloons, red silver,
flash, pop, umbrella
opening, Willow's gold, smoke
on the water, parachute green,
blue, chartreuse, Purple Dragon,
touch of boom, boom, sizzle,
aerial symphony
fireflies, shooting stars,
alka seltzer, cherry
seltzer, pink champagne.
I'm newborn, airborne,
free, past guilt
at the enchantment,
that for him
meant bombardment.

The Ministry of Peace

I Am From

the rocks and shore,
of fishermen, lobster boats,

mornings that rise from
blackness over water.

I am from shell shock
impermeable days

he reached for safety
after Omaha Beach.

I am from kitchens close to her
warming something

milky and salty on the stove,
from clam flats, mackerel traps, gulls

cruising for cast offs,
from moonlight through cedars

scraping bedroom windows
awake to long angry silences,

the suffering of a gentle
man made infantryman,

and a pearl, her shell worn
down to sand.

I am from a tense place, a scenic place,
a place where I hid and escaped
beyond the eight-room cape
stone-walled acres of hayfields

above a harbor of broken glass,
fear and laughter ground smooth

by tidal movement,
waves coming in, going out.

Moon Slide

My mother sometimes rides with me
        down the old oak banister,
                our shadows moon-sewn

close, her loose blue dress
        clover-flecked, my slacks
                frictionless

she asks if Dad got his wood in.
        "He's fine, he's alone,
                he eats lunches out

when he can see to drive.
        I wish he'd mention
                your name."

Astride the scalloped banister,
        she reminds me I once flew
                down over these stairs,

I was sure I could fly,
        that one day I'd take us above
                the toll of my father's war.

She smells of cinnamon
        as I lean into her, sail down
                the moon-chosen railing

her dress bellied,
        my legs free.

Shoreline

And when life is tumultuous,
this Point, its fierce undertows,
its jagged rocks that rise up
like plates on end
lures
me to breathe in
the wrestled air,
to follow dirt paths
through rosa rugosa
and white yarrow down

to the deep granite
crevices where I hide
as my daughter counts
to one hundred, ready or not.
The ocean cries on all sides
as it did when the first Blaisdells
in the *Angel Gabriel* washed
ashore in a hurricane, 1635.

Is it the quiet
in the moment between
the waves' thrash
that calms me,
or the history,
or the voice of the ocean
that always,
always returns.

Salmo, GMO

how you have leaped times out of mind
    —Yeats

The stream shivers silver,
        glimmering moonbeams
                from beneath a restless surface

muscling miles
        against elevation, against current
                to get this far, and not yet home.

Cast upstream, grapple back,
        I tell my son our desire must match
                theirs, set the hook

against sheer propulsion,
        against salmon will, hunger
                to mate, to spawn on natal ground.

But on first cast he snags a modified one.
        Little resistance, no fierce grace,
                all hunter prey. I don't say,

too easy. To him this is wild,
        infertile Nephthys escaping the marine lab,
                scales, dull wafers of light,

salmon's serrated teeth, saw-pit jaw,
        but ocean pout genes
                for year-round gorging

this fish he raises by caudal fin
        in triumph—*I caught it!*
                We stand knee-deep

in the fitful stream,
        at the feet of a stone staircase,
                in the rush of current

flowing against
        the pure silver blue
                leapers.

Snow Travels

light and down
in its kingdom

sweeps parallel
as supine you gaze,

question why remain,
and miss the great escape

south or west
still braced against

last week's freeze
that wheezes, moans

bone scrapes bone
until at once unleashed

into white silence
you travel as wind crystals

over neighbor's blue van
abandoned, up to its wheels

in white, over roofless shed
left open to soft fragments

falling over the woodpile
lining the drive

lighting on fir saplings
bowed down and higher,

birches regal parchment
cleaving and even these

peeled, dried,
crowned.

Stacking Wood

Afternoons, after the day's
flame burns down to ash
and wind, after setting
the gardens to rest as the sun
narrows its angle, its flight
equaling night, this month
once swollen with wagonloads
of mown hay, crisping light
now half-shadowed
by the eleventh.
I tackle the woodpile,
mound drying since early spring,
fire-lengths of maple, ash, birch,
one thick chunk,
that's all it takes to start,
that's all my arms can hold.

The first row on pallets for airflow,
coarse, split, no two wedges
the same, but fitted
between two rock maples,
bookends against the drop of light
and months ahead when
it feels like it's all
coming down.

Smell of moss,
pepper, feel of leather,
splinters of sand.
Alone stacking bones
to last out the cold.
Comfort of stacking
between trees once keeping
my father's firewood
pausing chest high,

spying the iron wagon wheel
rusting against the shed, I lift it
onto the shelf of hardwood,
making a window through the woodpile,
framing in the silence of the mountains.
A look out onto the far pasture where
neighbor's Holsteins graze,

past the clapboard cape of the widow
who needs help getting her wood in.
I cinch in the view with winter's gold,
building round and higher
until it frames sky
purpling over stands of balsam
and cedar, green incense of winter,
softening this hardwood wall.

We Wanted Color Not to Matter

ten years after King marched, the country
not yet absorbing Indian and ivory,

East and West, spectrum of innocence.
We spun the globe, drawn as we were

from opposite poles: jungle and pine,
engineer and poet making railway

connections. We wanted color
not to matter Portland to Portland.

Measuring distance by the tracks
that lay ahead, by cribbage games

we played with acquaintances,
exchanging seats to the gentle rock,

the stop to stop. Smell of coal smoke,
day-old cologne. Passing barns, silos,

backyards of cities, the mobility one feels
on a train, an Agatha Christie mystique

the whistle and all aboard of it,
being in it together.

We wanted color not to matter
on the long ride, the slow ride,

in suspended time of understanding,
quantifying, associating

while grasses lifted their seed heads
from a stone ballast

that tied the rails, melding genes,
color, striking sparks

as steel moved across steel.

The Edge of the Gorge
Man is by nature a political animal
—Aristotle

Canyons between us we can't understand.
Tell me stranger at this political divide,
what thresholds you failed to cross,

what you lost, that there's more
than nothing between us.

Freedom of thought, soft as Lambs-ear,
cashmere, fragrant as thyme-walked
ground. Somewhere between love & hate,

atheist & saint. Even Tolstoy wrote first of war.
Peace falls like spring rain, an eagle feather.

Tell me neighbor of thresholds you failed
to cross, what you lost, that there's more
than nothing between us.

"Can you divide this apple into three halves?"
your daughter asked, feeding other hungry mouths

as she opened hers. Division as portioning.
Peace drops like a whisper between prairie warbler
and lark bunting, one feeder, tern and gull, one shore,

low tide and high. Over mountains, plains, drop
all your thoughts, friend, until edges give way, tell me
of thresholds you failed to cross, what you lost,

that there's more than nothing between us. I'm wary
watching the broad-winged hawk circle, dive & rise.

Let stones shake from the ground up.
I want to feel the lift of your breath
on my cheek as you speak.

Chiang Mai, City of Temples

Gold domes, gold painted entryways,
shoeless crossings over white stones

past novice monks in orange robes
exploring their beliefs, as did Siddhartha,

as the *maha-thera* here teaches
untrained minds: *On knees, bow*

three times. Seated, let rise thought,
emotion, smoke burning off.

Discomfort in shoulders, back,
Name it, he says, *paining, paining.*

I breathe through ache of stillness,
of striving to be more, effort-gain.

Become empty as your image in the mirror.
Scent of agarwood, waves of quiet,

a hundred reasons to move
from before closed eyes,

the silent gold statue,
teacher who had first to walk

away from suffering
to find freedom

seated in selflessness.
"See you on the other side,"

said the driver of the hired motorbike
dropping me off the day

I entered the temple.

Take To The Streets, February 15, 2003

I wish I could shut up, but I can't, and I won't.
        —Desmond Tutu

Is it dangerous, she asked
exiting the bus against ten degree gusts,
walking Manhattan's Third Avenue,
dark casement awaking like Rembrandt
stroked the morning,
our numbers multiplying,
spilling into Second with neglected appeals.
                    Sure we were all mad
after the attacks, shocked back,
but what had these people done?
Wives of firefighters waved banners: *No blood for Oil*,
businesspeople, blue-collared, poor, frayed, disabled,
babies in strollers, Grace Paley, Susan Sarandon,
Desmond Tutu. 9/11 Families for Peaceful Tomorrows,
Half a million strong, said the man behind us
as we merged onto First, *The reports will pinch it,*
        say we're hippies, lefties,
gut our numbers. His suit had ridden many buses—
they always turn down the volume.
The world marched that day
against a rampage that would
yield no chemicals or Al-Qaeda.
Those who've walked the street never again
see only pavement. *No*, my daughter later told friends,
It isn't dangerous to walk,
only to not say a word.

Additional Acknowledgements:

With deep gratitude to Louise Rader, S.J. Cahill, the Wednesday Poets, the Northeast Storytellers, the Poetry Society of Vermont, and each of you who listened to and guided the path of these poems. I am forever indebted to Sylvia Field who opened the door to writing, and to the late Mame Willey who brought poetry into the room.

CPSIA information can be obtained
at www.ICGtesting.com
Printed in the USA
BVHW031449280119
538860BV00001B/66/P